pages of sunbeams

Joyful, Singable Rhymes to Brighten your Day

Written by **Mechelle Foster**

FREILING
PUBLISHING

Published by Freiling Publishing, a division of Freiling Agency, LLC.

P.O. Box 1264, Warrenton, VA 20188

www.FreilingPublishing.com

ISBN 978-1-956267-96-9

Printed in the United States of America

Dedication

This book is a collection of poems dedicated to and inspired by God and the children He has placed in my life- some of them, grown.

I began working with children when I was 16, and when I was almost 20, I married a children's pastor. My husband, Grant and I pastored kids for over two decades before becoming lead pastors at our church. Our most crucial pastoring role, however, has always been pastoring our own two children: Morgan and Zachary.

When my kids were very young, I was a stay-at-home mom. Although the unofficial slogan for The Peace Corps is, "The toughest job you'll ever love!" these words also apply to motherhood.

The days (and nights) of motherhood are often taxing, long and lonely. You learn to be creative and inventive when you're home all day with a one-year-old who has their own language, and an iron will. You also learn to cling to optimism, because utter despair lurks around every leaking sippy cup and potty seat.

It was during this wonderful, trying time I began to use rhyme to help teach and encourage my children. With each new experience or challenge came a new jingle. We sang and rhymed our way through the day. We sang about the sun in the morning, the foods we ate at noon and the Lord's watchful care before going to sleep at night. Now, I am the nana of two precious, little boys who are also constantly inspiring me. Many of the poems in this book are about them.

I would love to know why you decided to pick up this book. Was it because you follow my blog, *Rhyme, Reason & Real Life* and are familiar with my poetry? If you aren't currently following my blog, you can find me at mechellefoster.com.

Maybe you are a family member or friend who has always encouraged my pursuits. Choosing this book is another shake of your pom poms- not just any pom poms, the glittery, metallic ones with two colors. Thank you for cheering me on. I am thankful.

Perhaps you are a parent, teacher or student choosing books at a library or bookstore and this book simply caught your eye.

It could be, you're a writer yourself and long to publish a children's book one day.

Whatever the reason you are reading this, I hope this book brightens your day. I hope it will reconnect you with joy, hope and the wonder of childhood. I hope it makes you laugh and dance and sing. I hope it inspires you to write poetry and stories of your own. But most importantly, I hope it points you to Father God, the maker of sunbeams.

Have a sunny day,
Mechelle

Hopscotch Ocean

Ring toss river
Racoon stew
Hopscotch ocean
Purple emus

Checkers in my bathtub
Possums in my shoes
Let's clap!

Jump rope puddles
Jack rabbit pie
Hide and seek ocean
Cheetahs swimming by

Polka dotted blankie
Zebras in the sky
Let's dance!

Monkey bar creek
Turkey goose gumbo
Make believe ocean
Full of alphabets and numbos

I like this silly rhyme
Even though it's mumbo-jumbo
Let's hop!

Now stop!

Don't want this to end?
Then read it again...

Beach Baby

The ocean sees me
I'm so big
The gulls hear me singing
The sand feels me dig
The seaweed smells my nose
The salty waves taste my toes
I make the beach happy
The sun told me so!

Sandy Peach Tea

Sandy, peach tea
Come and drink a glass with me
By the waves of the ocean or the sea

Nothing tastes better
In this kind of weather
Than a glass of sandy, peach tea

You can't buy it from a store
When we run out, we make more
Of this wonderful, sandy, peach tea

My grandson taught me how
And I can make it now
Glorious, sandy, peach tea

To make it really grand
You'll need a toddler and some sand
And of course, a glass of peach tea

Just let the toddler be
Add some curiosity
And soon you'll have sandy, peach tea

Sandy, peach tea
Come and drink a glass with me
By the waves of the ocean or the sea

Nothing tastes better
In this kind of weather
Than a glass of sandy, peach tea

Child of Summer

Runnin' around barefoot

Makin' mud pies

Eatin' salted watermelon on the front porch, feet danglin'

Suntannin' on the roof of an old, broken-down Chevy

Drinkin' ice-cold well water from a long-handled, tin dipper

Wadin' in the cool creek, trying not to slip, watching crawdads
wiggle in the deep end

Singin' radio hits at the top of my lungs

Mamaw givin' us each a dollar

Walkin' to the store with my cousins

Pickin' out penny candies for as long as it took: toffees, rootbeer
barrels, caramels, butterscotch disks and bubblegum

Mamaw, her head out the window, tryin' to catch a deep breath,
watchin' folks come and go

Baths in the washtub - the dirtiest went last

Pokin' holes in the lid of an old Mason Jar

Catchin' lightnin' bugs just before dark

Lyin' on a pallet on the floor next to Mamaw's bed watchin' the
jar of lightnin' bugs flash off and on until we drift off to sleep

Dedicated to my Mamaw Maggie, my Kentucky cousins and my
Uncle Leroy- a coal miner. He was the dirtiest.

Beach Mouse

Don't call me a rat
I'm a beach mouse
I don't live in an ordinary house
My oceanfront home is quite grand
I don't sleep in a field
But a castle on the sand
I don't ransack through rubbish
My cheese is imported
The word, "rat" implies my activities are sordid
Now that makes me laugh
And outrages my staff
Who wait on me tirelessly night and day
Choosing the best meats
And only the best morsels
Of colorful fruit and crudités
All placed on a tiny wooden tray
Yes, I am a beach mouse
Not ordinary vermin
I'll overlook your error
Because, of course, you're only human.

Car Picnic

Let's all have a car picnic
Right here inside the car
Though the beach is right outside
I'm happy where we are

Rainy skies won't spoil my day
I'll still run and jump and play
Here inside the car

Gampy, Nana and Mommy
Are here inside the car with me
I'm not buckled in my seat
'Cause Gampy parked the car

'Neath a tall, shady tree
I'm not buckled in my seat
'Cause Gampy parked the car

Nana brought some food to share
I'm not buckled
No one cares
'Cause Gampy parked the car

Cookies, melon and peach tea
And tortillas, just for me
All here inside the car

Mommy wipes my tears away
We'll come back another day
Then I'll run and jump and play
With sun and sand and waves.

Bananas

I love bananas
I love the color
Love the taste

I love bananas
I love to wipe'em on my face

I love bananas
And not a bite'll go to waste
When you give me a banana

I love bananas
Oh yes, my love for them is real
I love bananas
I wish that I could eat the peel

I love bananas
The best part of every meal
Is undoubtedly bananas

Oh yes, I love to eat bananas
Oh yes, I love to eat bananas!

Sweet Potato Baby

Nana
Makes
Sweet potato pie
For her little baby
With the big brown eyes

Nana
Makes
Sweet potato pie
For her little sweet potato baby

Nana
Makes
Lemon pie
For her little baby
When he starts to cry

Nana
Makes
Lemon pie
For her little lemon pie baby

Nana
Makes
Apple pie
For her little baby
Who's the apple of her eye

Nana
Makes
Apple pie
For her little apple pie baby

Nana
Makes
Sugar cream pie
For her little baby
So sweet, my, my

Nana
Makes
Sugar cream pie
For her little sugar cream baby

Nana
Makes
Pumpkin pie
For her little baby
Who waves bye-bye

Nana
Makes
Pumpkin pie
For her little pumpkin pie baby

For her little sugar
For her little pumpkin
For her little sweet potato baby!

Popsicles

Hooray, Hooray for popsicles
Yay, yay for popsicles
I'm gonna have a popsicle
Today, today today!

Hooray, Hooray for popsicles
Yay, yay for popsicles
I'm gonna have a popsicle
Today, today today!

What Does Baby See?

Pineapple, palm Tree
That's what baby sees
When he looks around in Nana's room

A freshly cleaned floor
Where baby can explore
When he crawls around in Nana's room

He sees two wooden birds
And music can be heard
When baby spends time in Nana's room

An altar where she prays
Where baby stands to play
With toys he brings to Nana's room

A pillow and a bed
Where baby lays his head
When reading a book in Nana's room

Nana's room is fun
But now the day is done
And it's night-night time in baby's room

Goodnight baby
God bless you!

Snuggles From Heaven

I can't get enough of your cuddles
I can't get enough of your love

Jesus sent you for me to snuggle
Straight from Heaven above

I can't get enough of your kisses
Your nose, your toes, your cheeks

I can't get enough of you cuddles, snuggles, kisses
You mean the world to me!

Little Hands Folded to Pray

Little hands folded to pray
Thanking the Lord for the food on his plate
For peaches and pears and apples and grapes
Little Hands folded to pray

Little hands folded to pray
Thanking the Lord at the end of the day
For mommy and daddy, every name he can say
Little hands folded to pray

Big hands folded to pray
Thanking the Lord throughout the day
For home and work and His help 'long the way
And for little hands folded to pray

Baby Brother

Mommy and Daddy brought me home a brother
I've seen babies before
But this one's like no other

Sure, he looks like babies do
He smells just like them too
Not to mention he's brand new
And he's sleeping in my room

But there's two little things that set him apart
The first is the way that I feel in my heart
The second is something I almost can't believe
This baby brother belongs especially to me!

Cuddly, Huggly, Ro

Cuddly, huggly, Ro
He's the sweetest baby I know

I like to kiss his cheeks
I like to tickle his toes

I like to say, "Goochie goo,"
The only words he knows

Oh, how I love him so
Cuddly, huggly, Ro

Heavy Bonnet

I tire so of this heavy bonnet
White and scratchy
Ruffles upon it

Why must my kin
Upon me gawk
With "goochy goo" and nonsense talk?

Kissing and pinching and bouncing me...
Why?
It's enough to make a baby cry!

Bear and Bunny

My favorite toys
Don't make noise
They don't have flashing lights

They are soft and fluffy
They are bear and bunny
And without them I can't sleep at night.

Mr. Curiosity

Hey there, Mr. Curiosity
Do you wanna come along with me?
There's a lotta fun things we can see
Mr. Curiosity

Momma's in the kitchen makin' breakfast for you
Let me pick you up for a better view
You can be a famous chef when you're two
Mr. Curiosity

Grammy's in the garden plantin' roses and trees
You love to watch her dig and hear the birdies sing
You can be a master gardener when you're three
Mr. Curiosity

Nana picks you up, you sway across the floor
The music ends, she puts you down and you shout, "More!"
You can be a ballroom dancer when you're four
Mr. Curiosity

Gampy's in the car, he has just arrived
You jump up in his lap so you can help him drive
You can be a famous racer when you're five
Mr. Curiosity

Hey there, Mr. Curiosity
You can be whatever you wanna be
I'll be there to cheer you on; count on me
Mr. Curiosity

Full of Beans

My nana says I'm full of beans
I have no idea what that means
I didn't eat beans for breakfast or lunch
Or dinner last night
Or Sunday Brunch
I most often eat peanut butter and jelly
I'm quite certain that's what you would find in my belly.

Me and You and Gampy

It's just me and you and Gampy on the couch
Oh, yes, we're the only people in the house
We can make a lot of noise
Play with all your favorite toys
Just me and you and Gampy on the couch

It's just me and you and Gampy in the car
We'll set out with the sun
And come home with the stars
There'll be music in between
And maybe ice cream bars
Just me and you and Gampy in the car

It's just me and you and Gampy at the zoo
We'll visit all the monkeys, the birds and zebras too
Black and white pandas and the baby kangaroos
Just me and you and Gampy at the zoo

It's just me and you and Gampy on the couch
Oh, yes, we're the only people in the house
The toys are put away
It was such a happy day
Mommy and Daddy on the way
Until then, asleep we'll stay
Just me and you and Gampy on the couch.

Asher Grey

How I love you, Asher Grey
Love all the words you say
I don't always understand you, but I'm sure I will someday
Asher Grey

How I love you, Asher Grey
Love to watch you run and play
To try and pick up Emma just before she runs away
Asher Grey

How I love you, Asher Grey
Love you in every way
I love to read you stories at the end of the day
Asher Grey

He Licked the Dog

He licked the dog.

He's only 10 months old
And apparently was never told
Not to lick the dog.

Happy together
They run and play
And I've never heard his mother say,
"Don't lick the dog!"

He can't feed the dog
Or throw her toy
I guess the expression of his joy
Was to lick the dog.

I've seen the dog lick his face
It's only fair he should reciprocate
And lick the dog.

Do you agree? Or is it just me?

Riding with Doggie

There's a doggie in my seat
And I think it's really neat
And I never want to ride alone again

With a doggie next to me
I'm as happy as can be
Is that why they call him man's best friend?

Alpha-pet

Amazing
Boston Terrier
Cat-
Dog
Emma is
Fun
Good-
Hearted
Intelligent
Jumps high
Kisses babies
Likes bananas
Makes strangers nervous
Naps often
Outside if possible
Playful sometimes
Quiet mostly
Ravenous eater
Suspicious of vacuums and mops
Toddler approved
Up on the couch is her guilty pleasure
Vicious? Never!
Watchdog? Always!
X-plorer? Definitely!
You must also know
Zoomies are her specialty.

Cat-Dog-Hog

My dog Emma is a cat-dog-hog.

She's a dog that acts like a cat.
She's skittish, aloof and other feline things like that.

She's a dog by design-
She plays fetch and loves her bones,

But don't try to pet her,
She would rather be alone.

But if you stand in the kitchen, banana in your grip
She will suddenly appear.
Be careful, you might trip

As she springs from the trap door
Hidden just beneath your feet
And just like that, she's ready to eat.

"No, Emma, you can't eat all the bananas," I say.
What a hog!
And that's why I call her a cat-dog-hog.

Nobody Hates You, Emma

Nobody hates you, Emma
Even though you act like a cat!

Nobody hates you, Emma
And you can be sure about that!

Even though we wanna love you, Emma
To hold you and pet you, Emma

You walk away
You're a dramatic dog
Here's a dramatic song
For you

Emma
Emma
We just want to love you, Emma.

Love Your Brother

I would never kill my brother
I would never spike his tea
I would never kill my brother
Even though he's mean to me

He kicks me in the stomach
He bites me on the knee
But I would never, no never
Kill my brother

God wants you to love your brother
So, here's what you must do
You must love your brother
Just as much as you love you

And if you are discouraged
There's one thing you don't do
Never, no, never kill your brother

'Cause your brother is another man
Living here upon this land
God is the one who gave him life
And you don't have the right God has
So, if your brother makes you mad
You still don't have the right to pick him off

Now the moral of my story
Is put away your wrath
Please don't kill your brother
Or put his name on an epitaph

Now you might think I'm silly
And I might even make you laugh
But never, no, never, kill your brother.

When the Sun Comes Up

The bird on the wire watches the sun
Before it flies away to start the day

I watch the bird as I wait for the sun
Here on the porch where I pray

God watches me, for He makes the sun rise
And the bird, though it's small, has also caught His eye

He cares for us both
And He always provides

Each day when the sun comes up.

Purpose

Why say, "It can't be done,"
Before you even try?

Behind those clouds are sunbeams
Let them brighten up your sky

Why stay here on the ground?
You could be soaring high

Spread those beautiful wings
You were meant to fly!

Oh, Glimmer of Light

Oh, glimmer of light, you are beautiful
I want to study you
Boldly, for a moment, I gaze at you
With spotted sight, I look away
Shielded by my hand, I turn back to you
Circle expanding
Influence growing
Higher and higher
Lighting and warming the earth as you rise.

Nature Walk

A pinecone in my pocket isn't particularly pleasant.
Searching for something softer, I see the sky.

Fleeing frantically from the fated forecast,
I come to a cavern, commonly called a cave.

Relieved, I rest-
The pinecone protected perfectly and painfully in my pocket.

Studying the sky as I sit, I see a solution to my suffering.
Rain relenting, I run from my refuge.

Hiking higher and higher,
Huffing and hoping I halt!

Near a nest I nobly kneel.
A freshly fallen feather
Will free me from my pinecone peril!

Storm Cadence

Look up in the sky
Everything is dark
I think it's gonna rain
I think it's gonna rain

Birds are flying fast
Above me in the park
I think it's gonna rain
I think it's gonna rain

Clouds fill the sky
I cannot see the sun
I think it's gonna rain
I think it's gonna rain

Drip drop
Drip drop
Drip drop
Run!

It's raining!
It's raining!
It's raining!

www.ingramcontent.com/pod-product-compliance
Lightning Source LLC
Chambersburg PA
CBHW042001100426
42813CB00019B/2952